Compositions
for Renaissance Lute

Matthew Leigh EMBLETON (b1978)

Copyright ©2020 Matthew Leigh Embleton. All rights reserved.

Compositions for Renaissance Lute

01 Journey in d-minor 4
02 Nocturnes in d-minor and e-minor 6
03 From Depth in a-minor 8
04 Nocturnes in f-minor and g-minor 9
05 Small Floating Crafts in c-minor 12
06 Journey in a-minor 16
07 Journey in c-minor 20
08 Nocturne in c-minor 26
09 Tasmanian Lake d-minor 28
10 Extransience in d-minor 30
11 Victoria Park, December 2005 in e-minor (Version 1) 31
11 Victoria Park, December 2005 in e-minor (Version 2) 32
12 Late Night Sky in g-minor 33
13 Introduction in g-minor 34

Acknowledgments

Thanks to Susan King, David Van Ooijen, Stuart Walsh, Steve Metcalfe, and Wezi Elliot for their feedback, collaboration, support, and encouragement.

Thanks to Luke Emmett and Christopher Goodwin, Stewart McCoy, Christopher Wilson, Shirley Rumsey, Richard Mackenzie, Taro Takeuchi, Zak Ozmo, Lynda Sayce, Brian Wright, Stephanie Feeney, Denys Stephens, and The Lute Society (https://www.lutesociety.org/)

Thanks to Matteo Simone, Francesco Tribioli, Gian Luca Lastraioli, Giorgio Ferraris, Franco Fois, Massimo Marchese, and the Società del Liuto (http://societadelliuto.it/)

Thanks to Catherine Liddell, Dan Larson, Nancy Carlin, and The Lute Society of America (http://lutesocietyofamerica.org/)

Thanks to the special people in my life who have supported and encouraged me in my work. Thank you for believing in me. You know who you are.

Matthew Leigh Embleton (b1978) Compositions for Renaissance Lute

Op 01 Journey in d-minor

01 Introduction, *piano con affetto*

02 The Pursuit, *con affetto e un poco agitato*

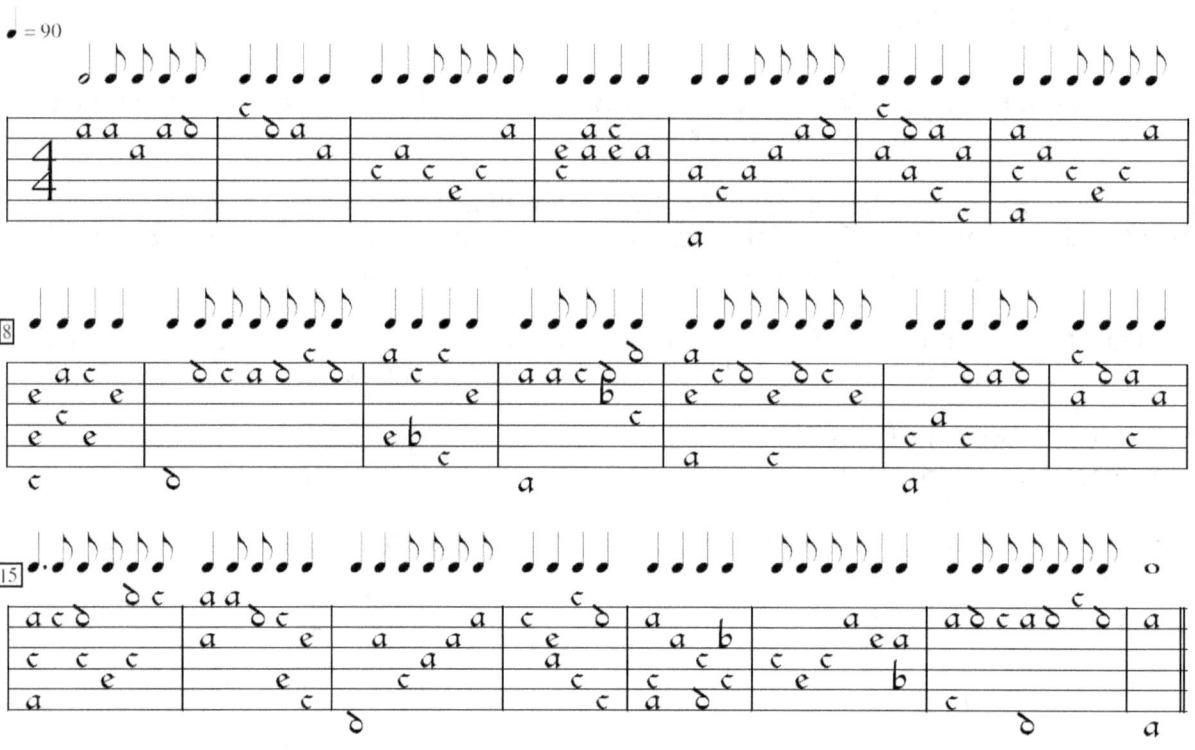

©2012, 2013, 2015, and 2020 Matthew Leigh Embleton

03 Looking Skyward, *con larghezza*

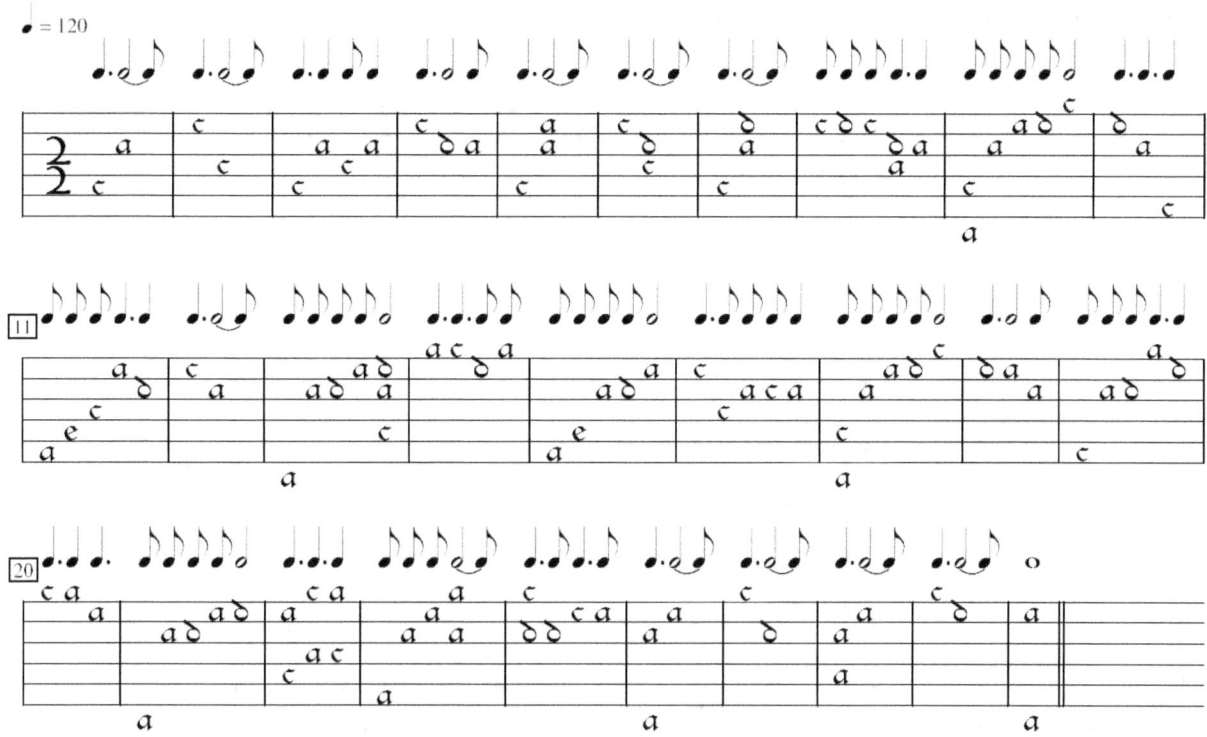

Matthew Leigh Embleton (b1978) — Compositions for Renaissance Lute

Op 02 Nocturnes in d-minor and e-minor

01 Nocturne in d-minor, *piano molto e cantabile*

©2012, 2013, 2015, and 2020 Matthew Leigh Embleton

Matthew Leigh Embleton (b1978) — Compositions for Renaissance Lute

02 Nocturne in e-minor, *piano molto e cantabile*

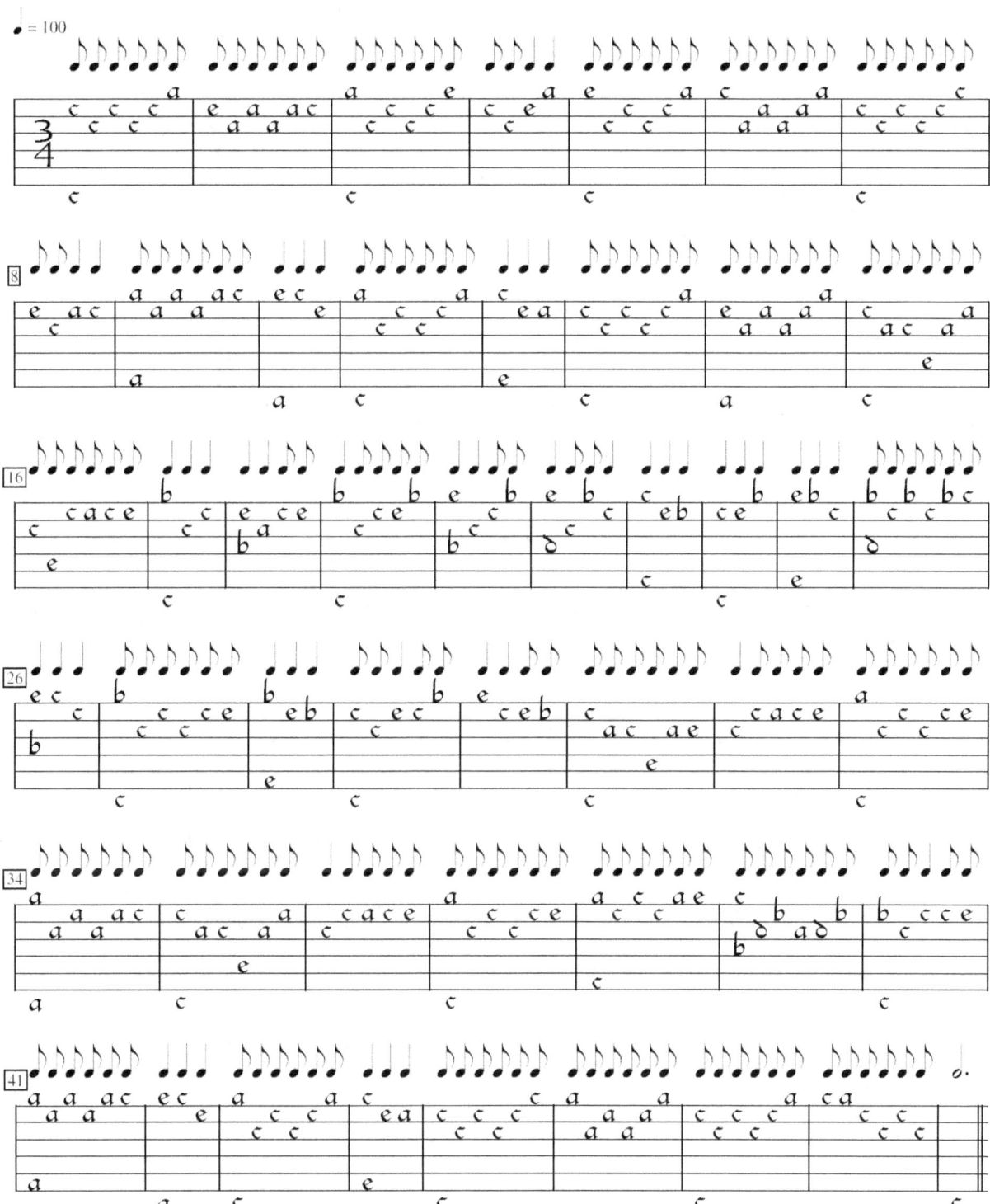

©2012, 2013, 2015, and 2020 Matthew Leigh Embleton

Matthew Leigh Embleton (b1978) — Compositions for Renaissance Lute

Op 03 From Depth in a-minor

Piano molto e penseroso

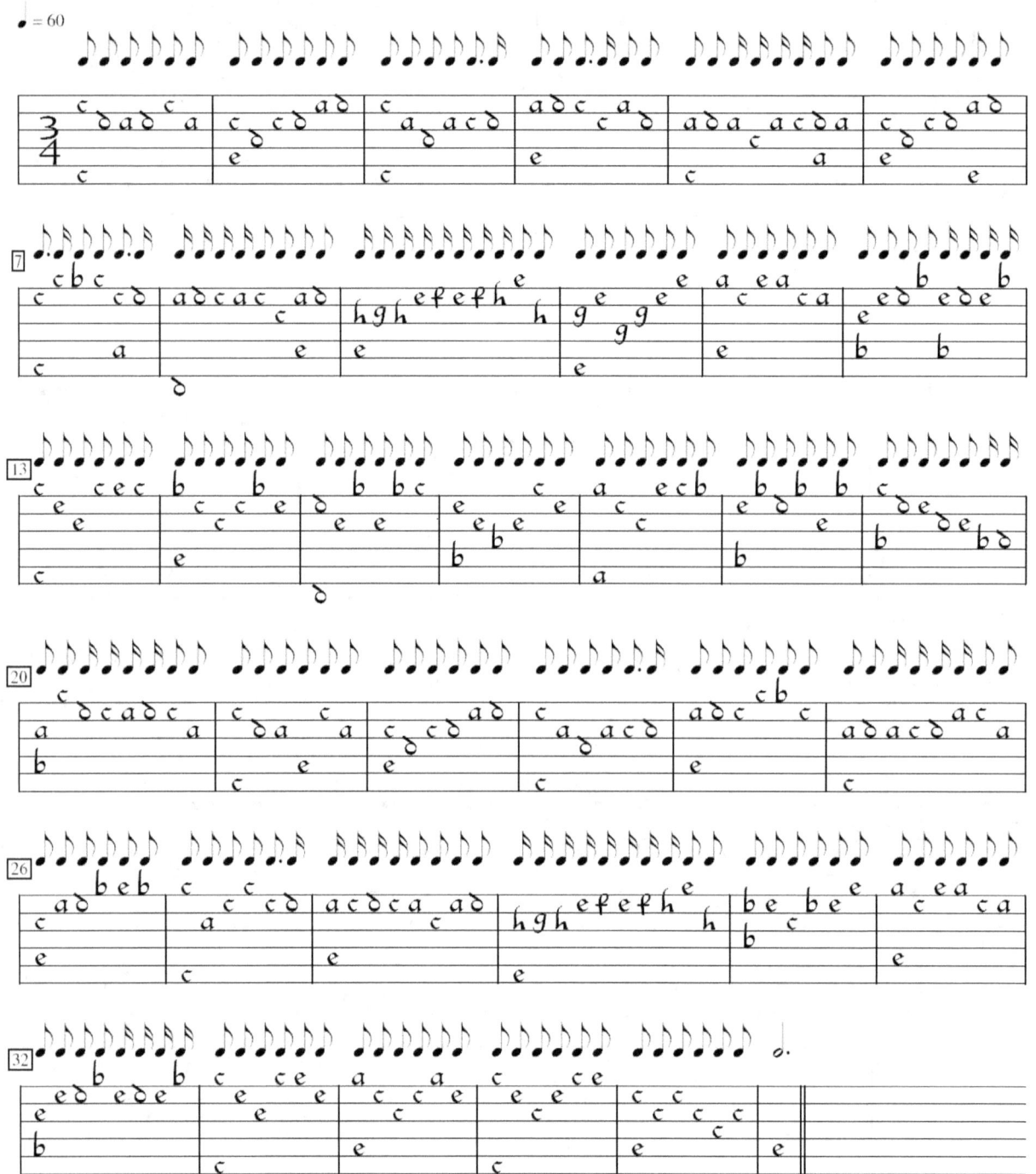

©2012, 2013, 2015, and 2020 Matthew Leigh Embleton

Op 04 Nocturnes in f-minor and g-minor

01 Nocturne in f-minor, *piano molto e cantabile*

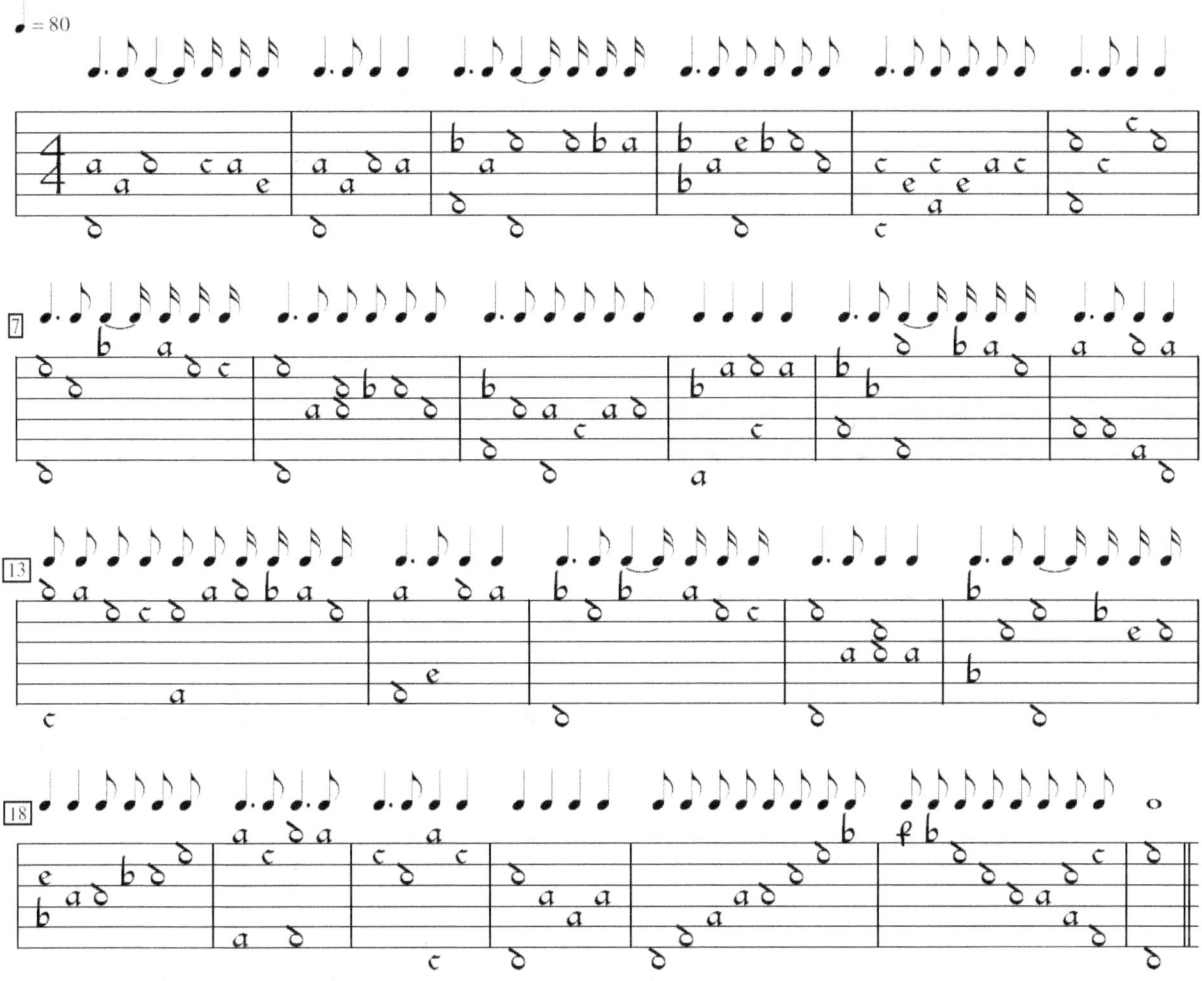

©2012, 2013, 2015, and 2020 Matthew Leigh Embleton

Matthew Leigh Embleton (b1978) — Compositions for Renaissance Lute

02 Nocturne in g-minor (Version 1), *piano molto e cantabile*

©2012, 2013, 2015, and 2020 Matthew Leigh Embleton

Matthew Leigh Embleton (b1978) — Compositions for Renaissance Lute

02 Nocturne in g-minor (Version 2), *piano molto e cantabile*

©2012, 2013, 2015, and 2020 Matthew Leigh Embleton

Matthew Leigh Embleton (b1978) — Compositions for Renaissance Lute

Op 05 Small Floating Crafts in c-minor

01 Introduction, *con rubato e improvvisazione*

02 Interlude, *con rubato e improvvisazione*

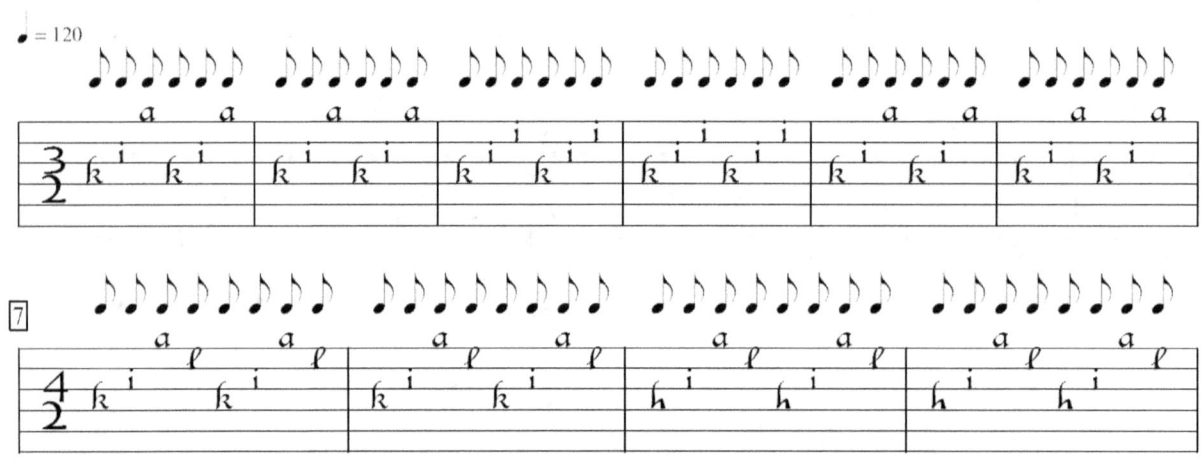

©2012, 2013, 2015, and 2020 Matthew Leigh Embleton

Matthew Leigh Embleton (b1978) — Compositions for Renaissance Lute

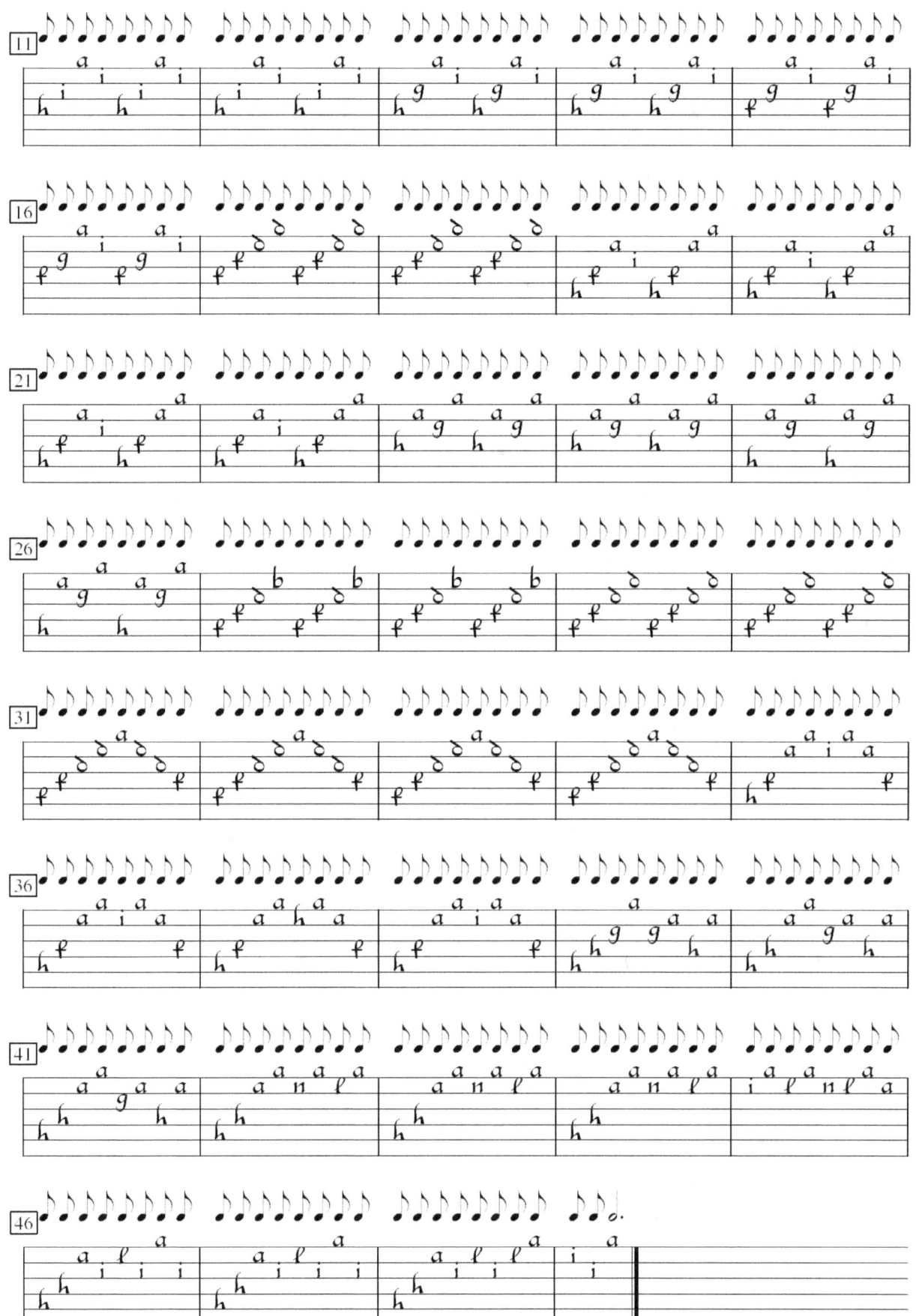

©2012, 2013, 2015, and 2020 Matthew Leigh Embleton

Matthew Leigh Embleton (b1978) — Compositions for Renaissance Lute

03 Conclusion, *con rubato e improvvisazione*

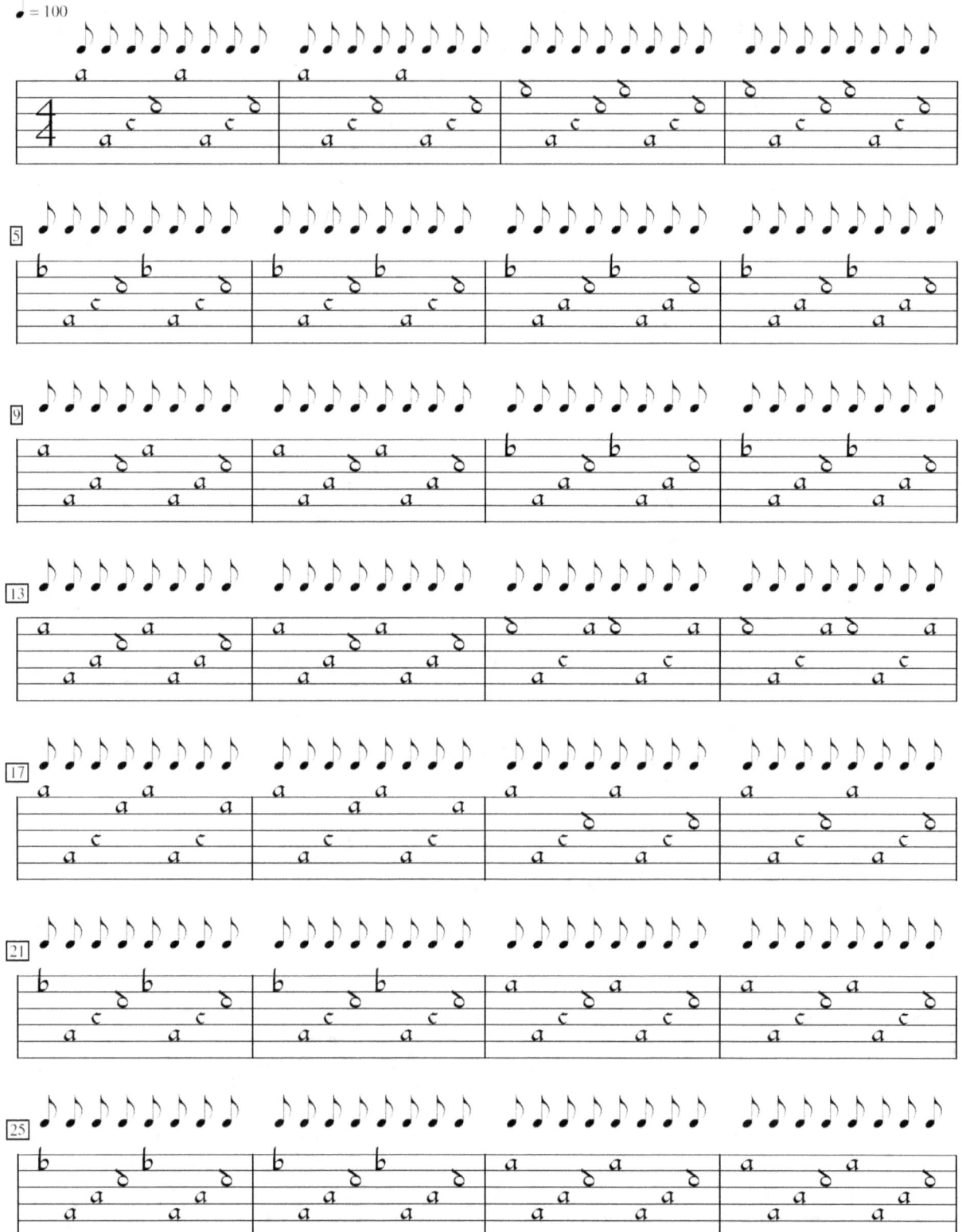

©2012, 2013, 2015, and 2020 Matthew Leigh Embleton

Matthew Leigh Embleton (b1978) — Compositions for Renaissance Lute

Matthew Leigh Embleton (b1978) — Compositions for Renaissance Lute

Op 06 Journey in a-minor

01 Arpeggiata, *adagio andante e piano*

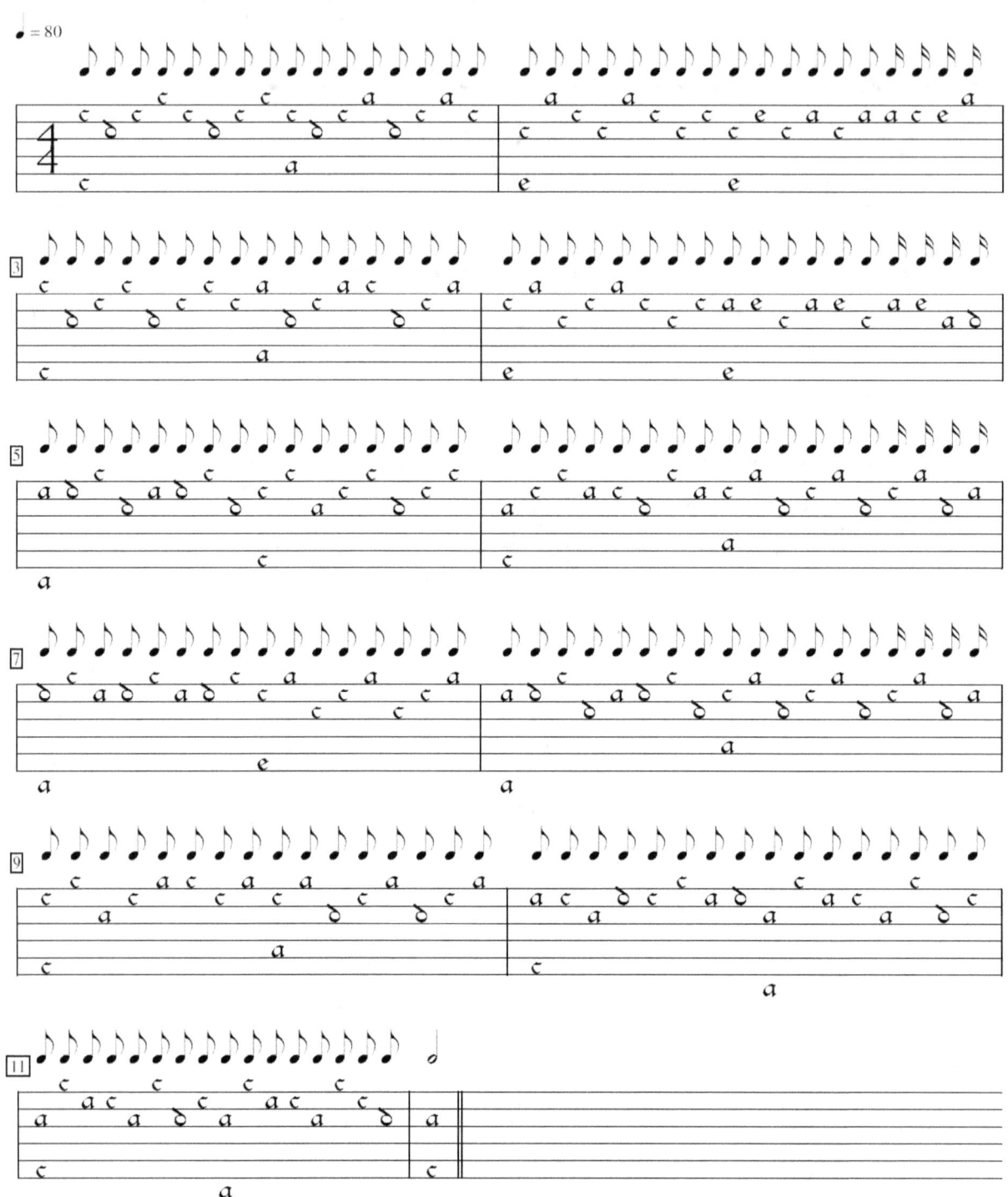

©2012, 2013, 2015, and 2020 Matthew Leigh Embleton

Matthew Leigh Embleton (b1978) Compositions for Renaissance Lute

02 Cloud Level (Version 1), *piano molto e penseroso*

02 Cloud Level (Version 2), *piano molto e penseroso*

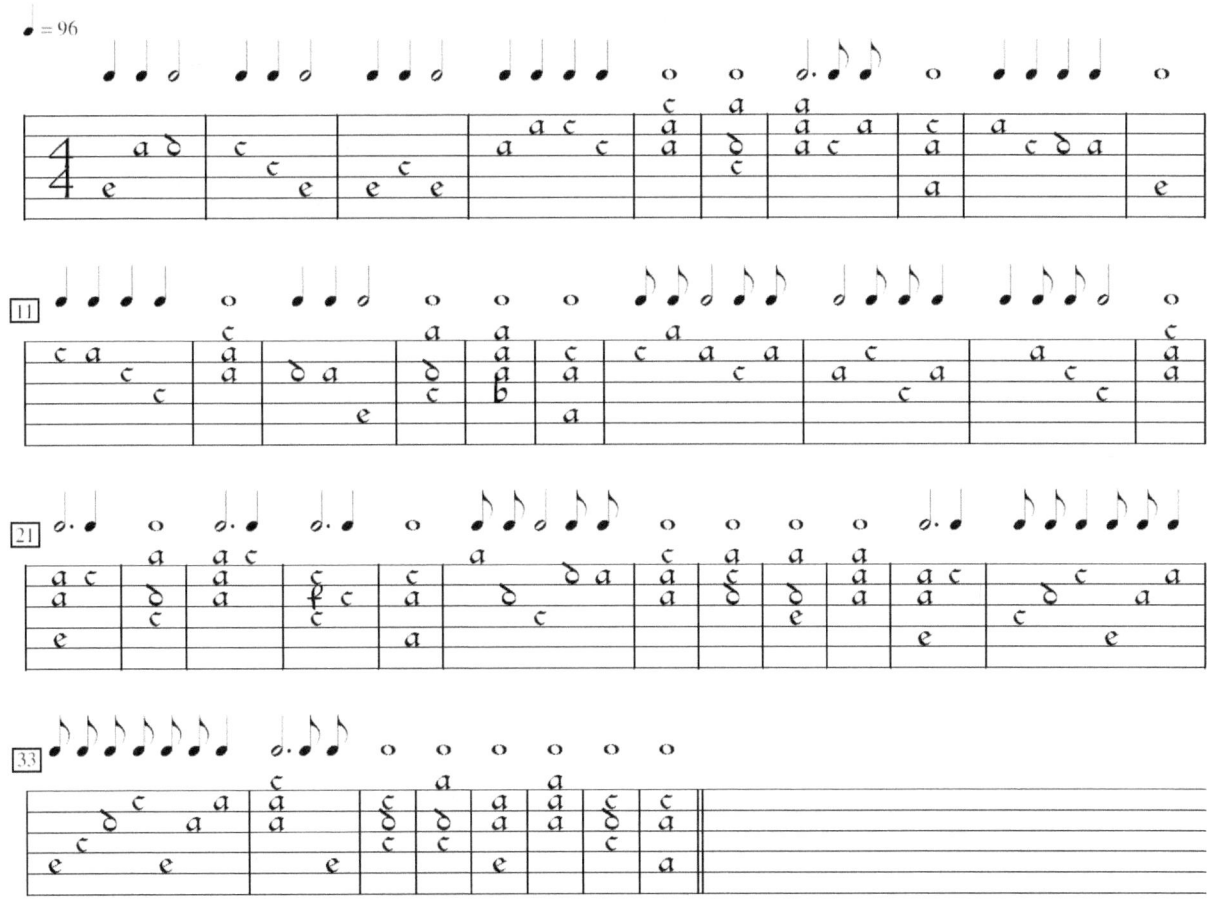

©2012, 2013, 2015, and 2020 Matthew Leigh Embleton

Matthew Leigh Embleton (b1978) — Compositions for Renaissance Lute

03 Eternal Recurrence (Version 01), *piano molto con affetuoso*

©2012, 2013, 2015, and 2020 Matthew Leigh Embleton

Op 07 Journey in c-minor

01 Introduction, *andante*

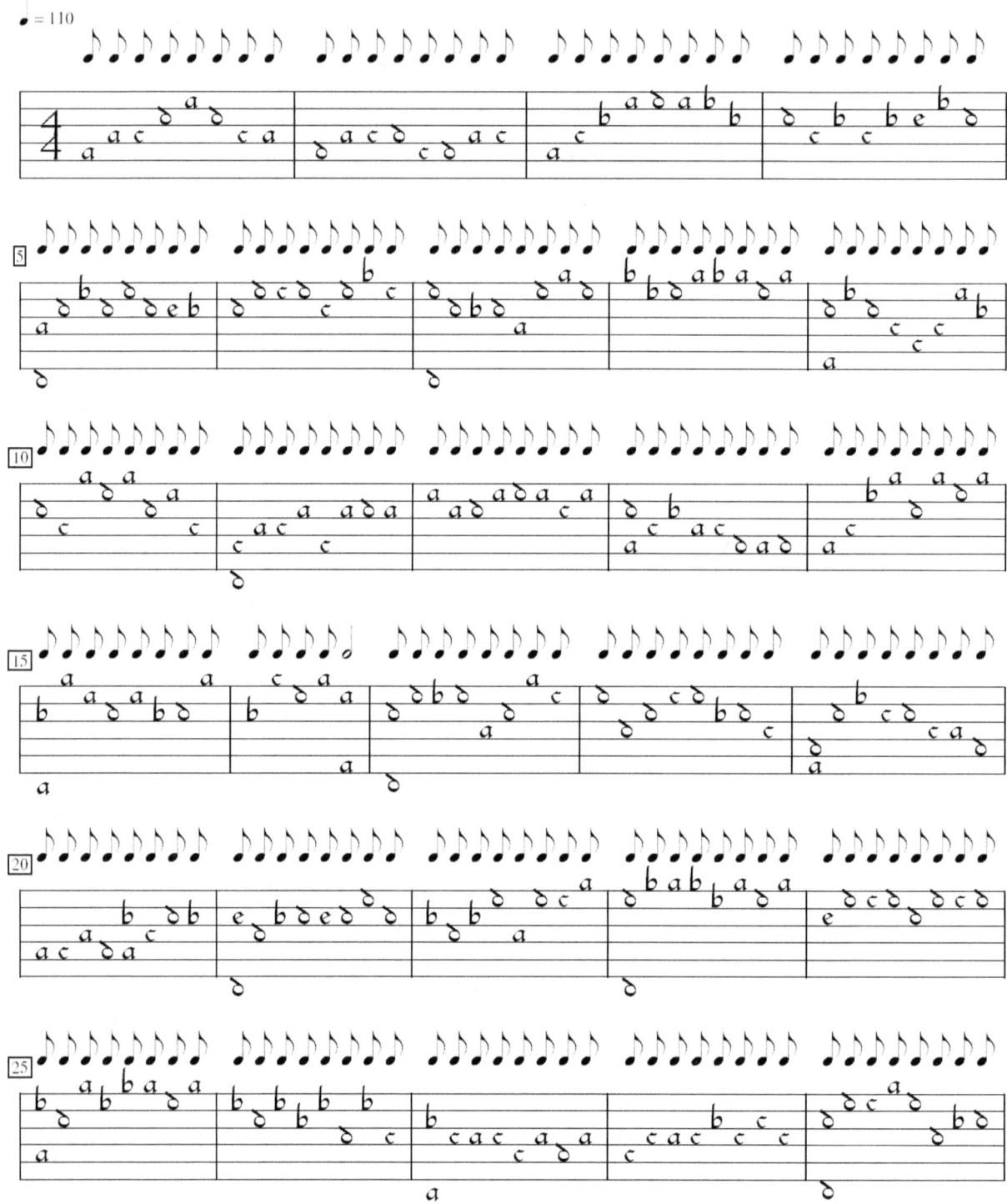

Matthew Leigh Embleton (b1978) — Compositions for Renaissance Lute

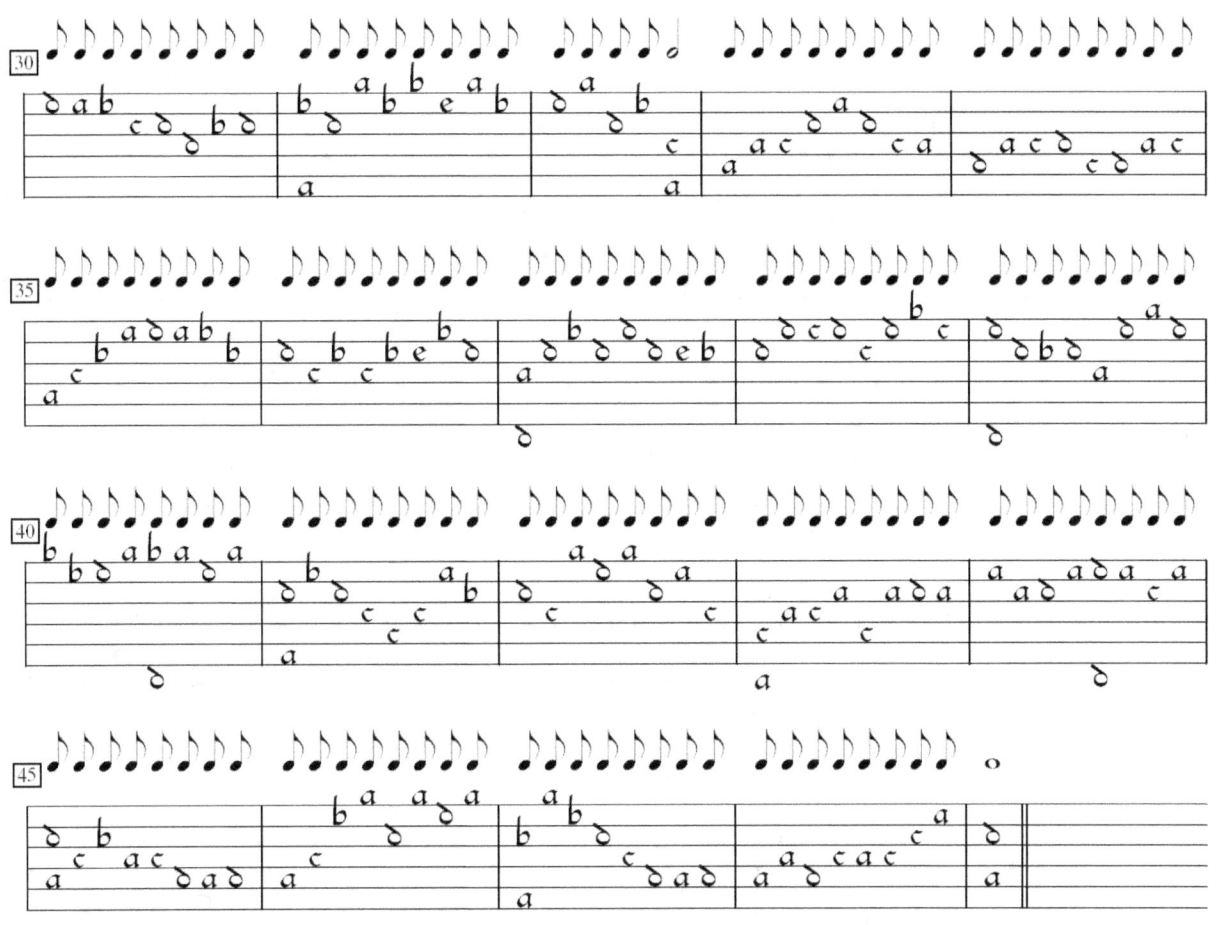

©2012, 2013, 2015, and 2020 Matthew Leigh Embleton

Matthew Leigh Embleton (b1978) — Compositions for Renaissance Lute

02 Interlude, *adagio*

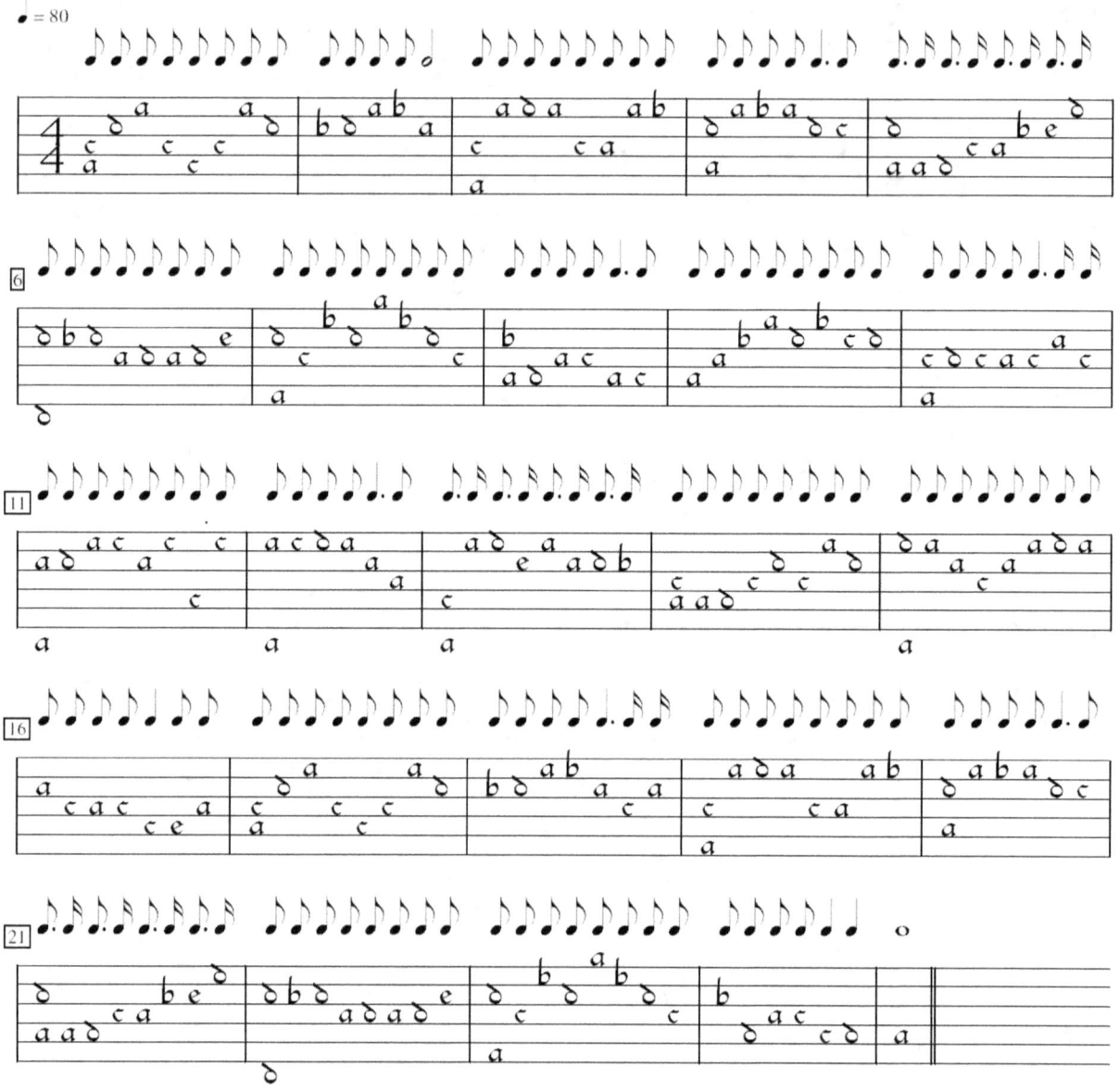

Matthew Leigh Embleton (b1978) — Compositions for Renaissance Lute

03 Conclusion, *allegro*

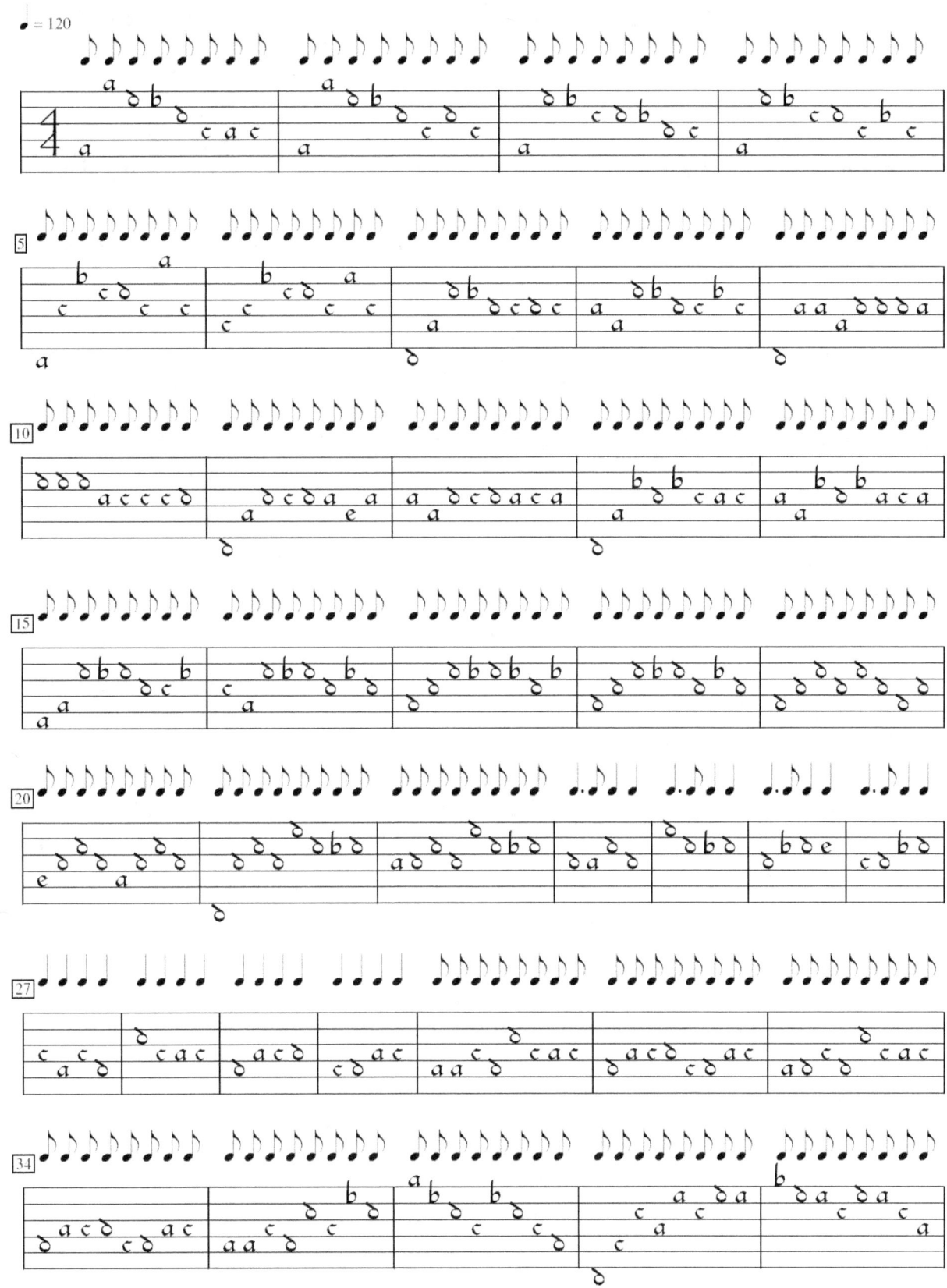

©2012, 2013, 2015, and 2020 Matthew Leigh Embleton

Matthew Leigh Embleton (b1978) — Compositions for Renaissance Lute

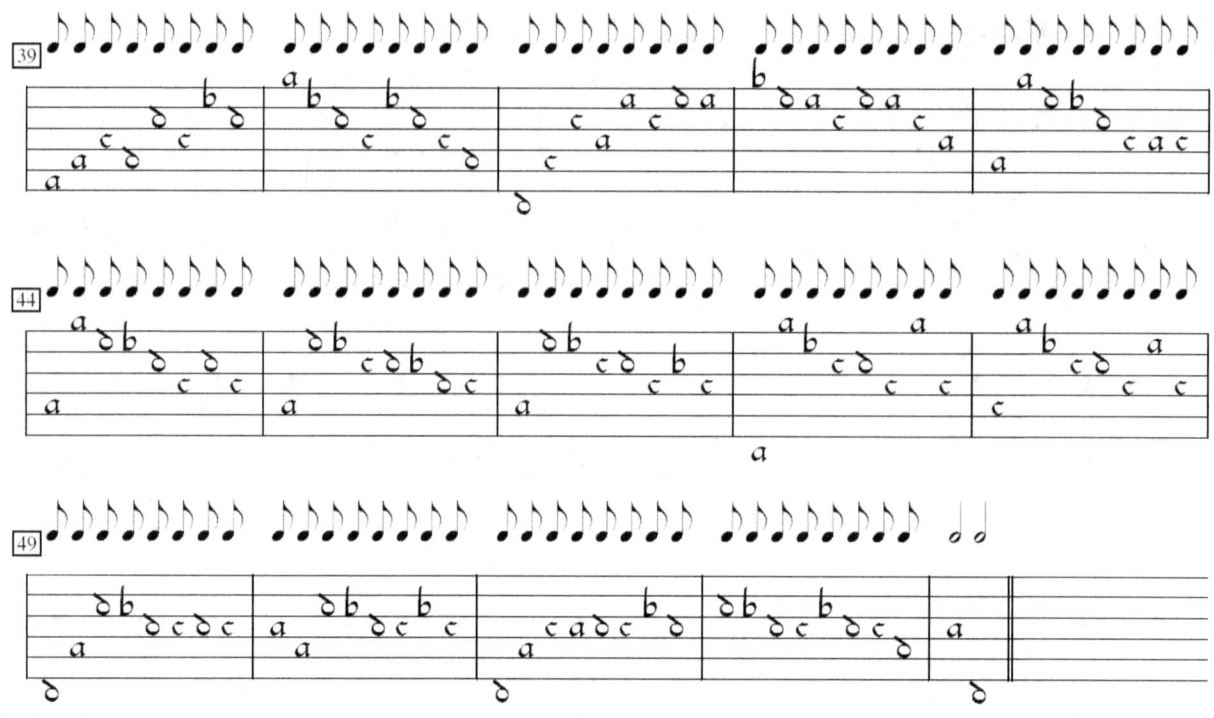

©2012, 2013, 2015, and 2020 Matthew Leigh Embleton

Matthew Leigh Embleton (b1978) — Compositions for Renaissance Lute

Op 08 Nocturne in c-minor

Piano molto e cantabile

Matthew Leigh Embleton (b1978) — Compositions for Renaissance Lute

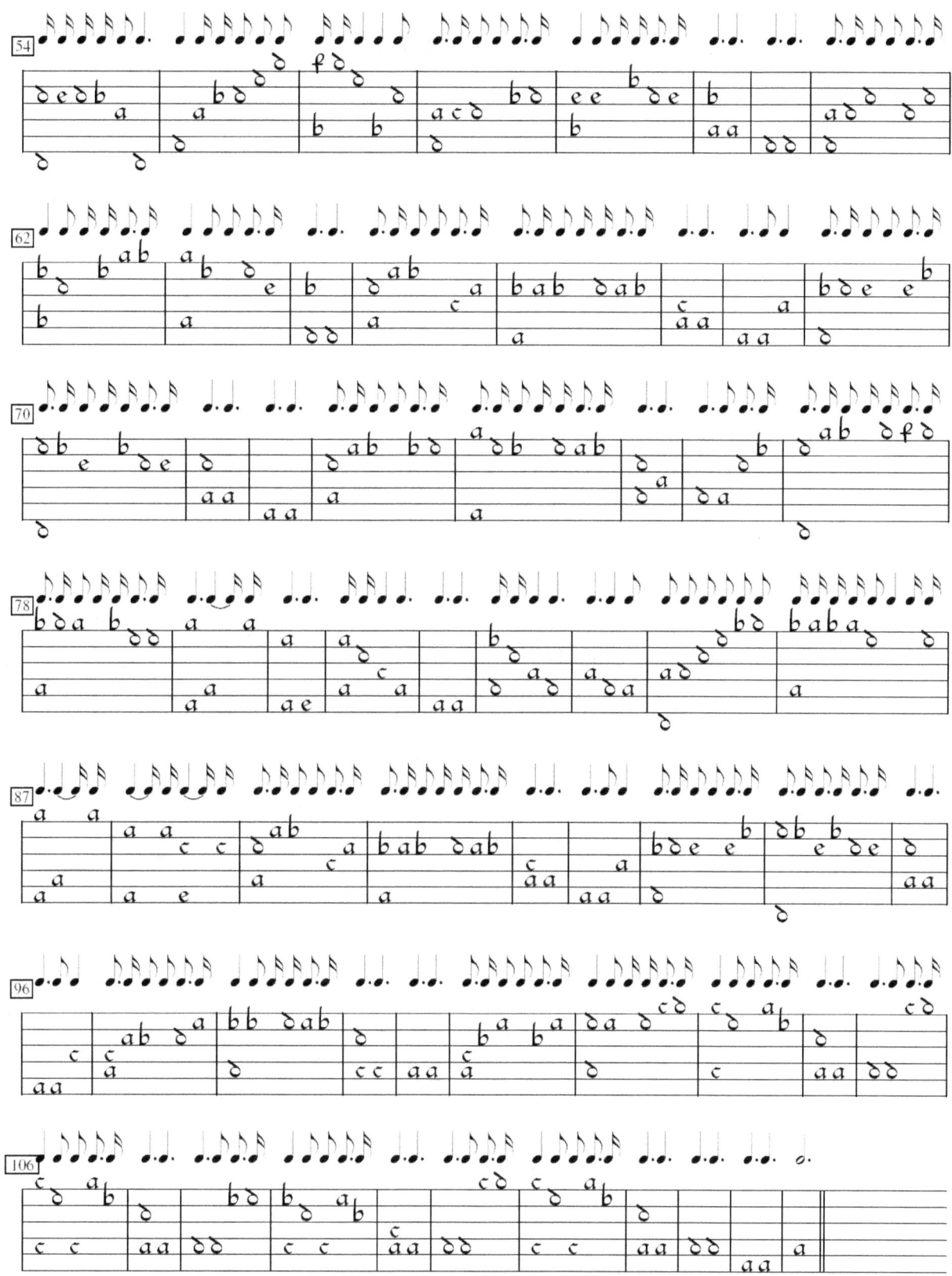

©2012, 2013, 2015, and 2020 Matthew Leigh Embleton

Matthew Leigh Embleton (b1978) — Compositions for Renaissance Lute

Op 09 Tasmanian Lake d-minor

Piano molto e penseroso

©2012, 2013, 2015, and 2020 Matthew Leigh Embleton

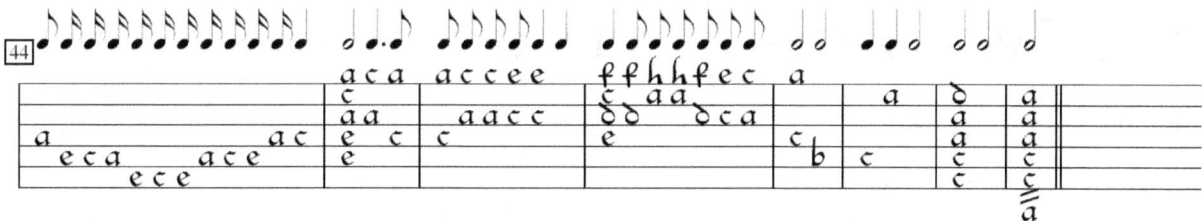

Matthew Leigh Embleton (b1978) — Compositions for Renaissance Lute

Op 10 Extransience in d-minor

Affrettando con poco agitato

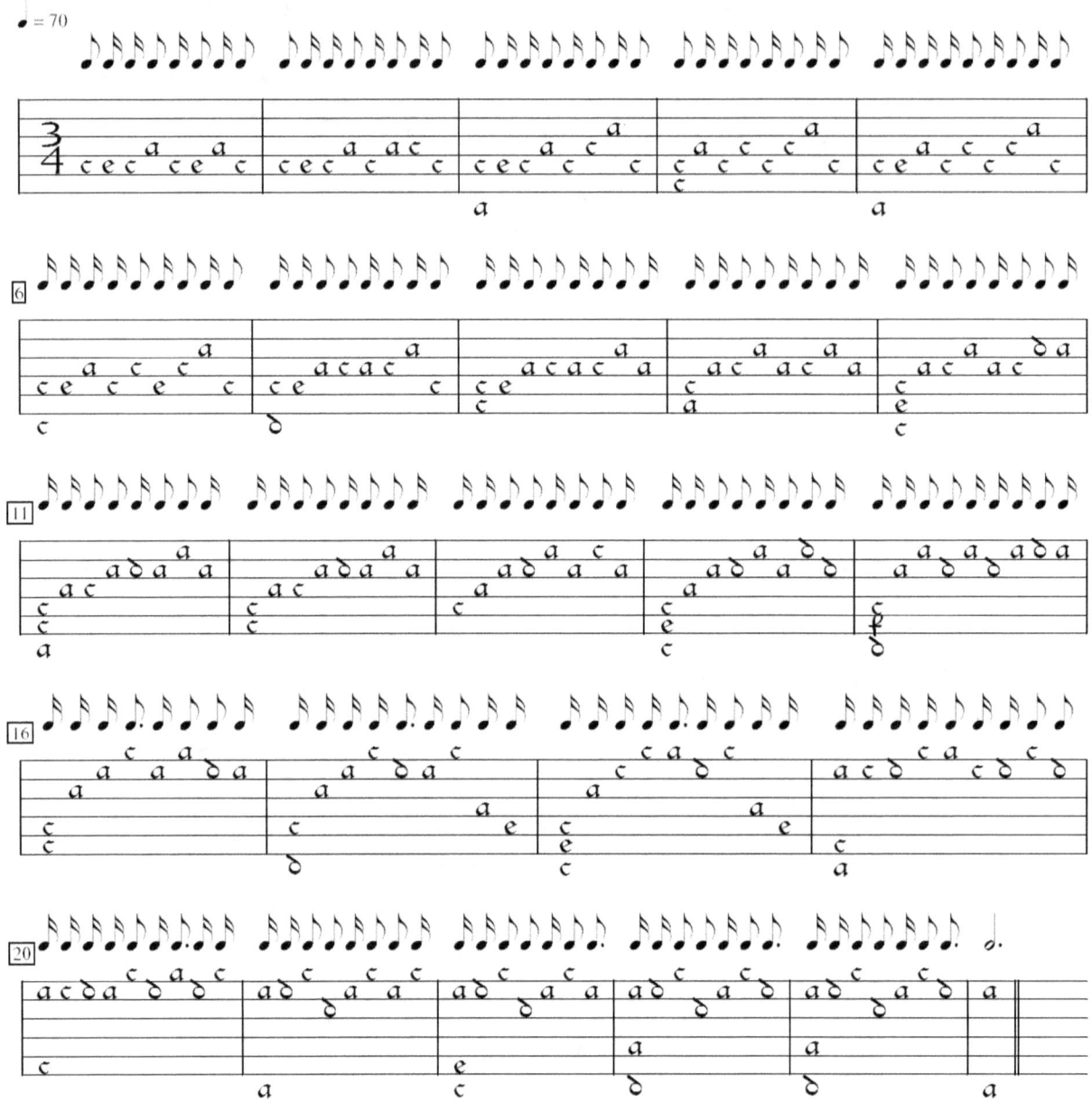

©2012, 2013, 2015, and 2020 Matthew Leigh Embleton

Matthew Leigh Embleton (b1978) — Compositions for Renaissance Lute

Op 11 Victoria Park, December 2005 in e-minor (Version 1)

Piano molto e penseroso

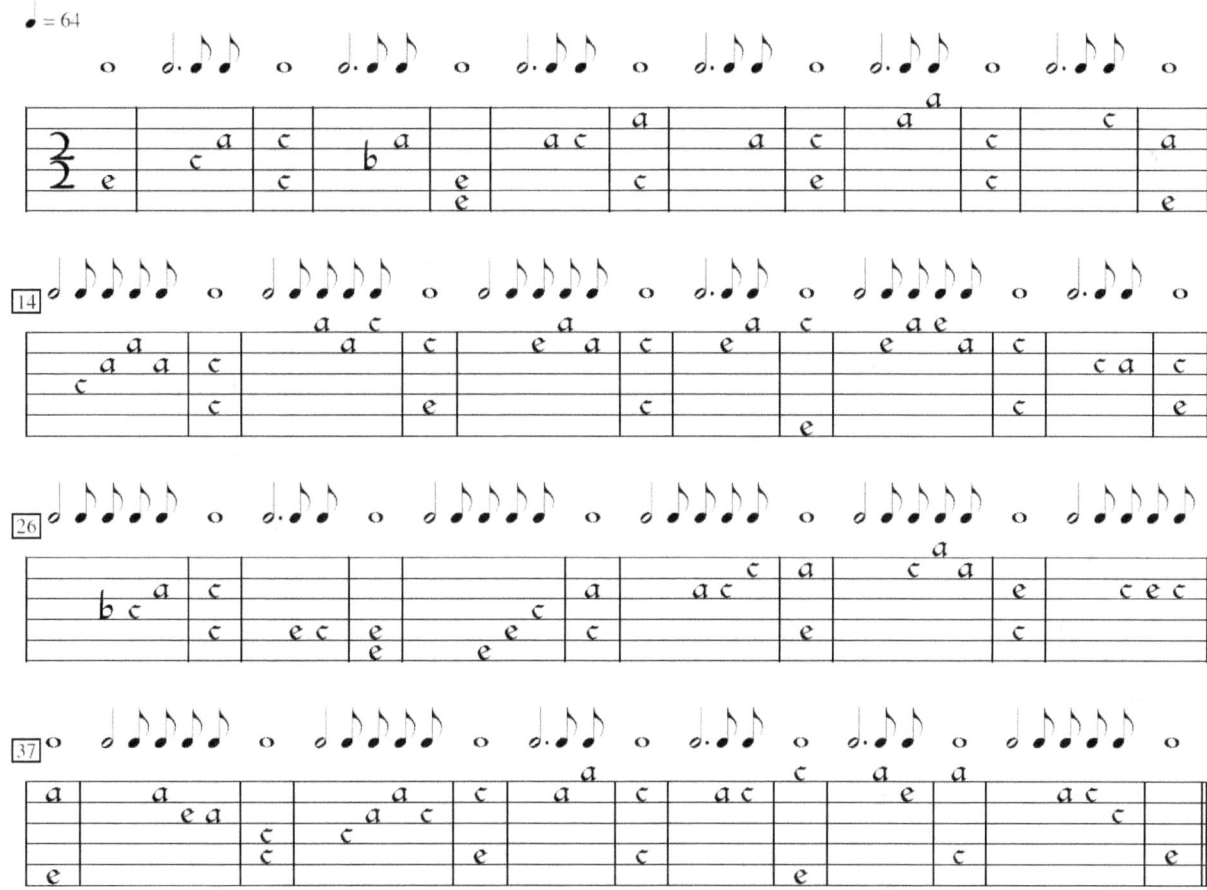

©2012, 2013, 2015, and 2020 Matthew Leigh Embleton

Matthew Leigh Embleton (b1978) Compositions for Renaissance Lute

Op 11 Victoria Park, December 2005 in e-minor (Version 2)

Piano molto e penseroso

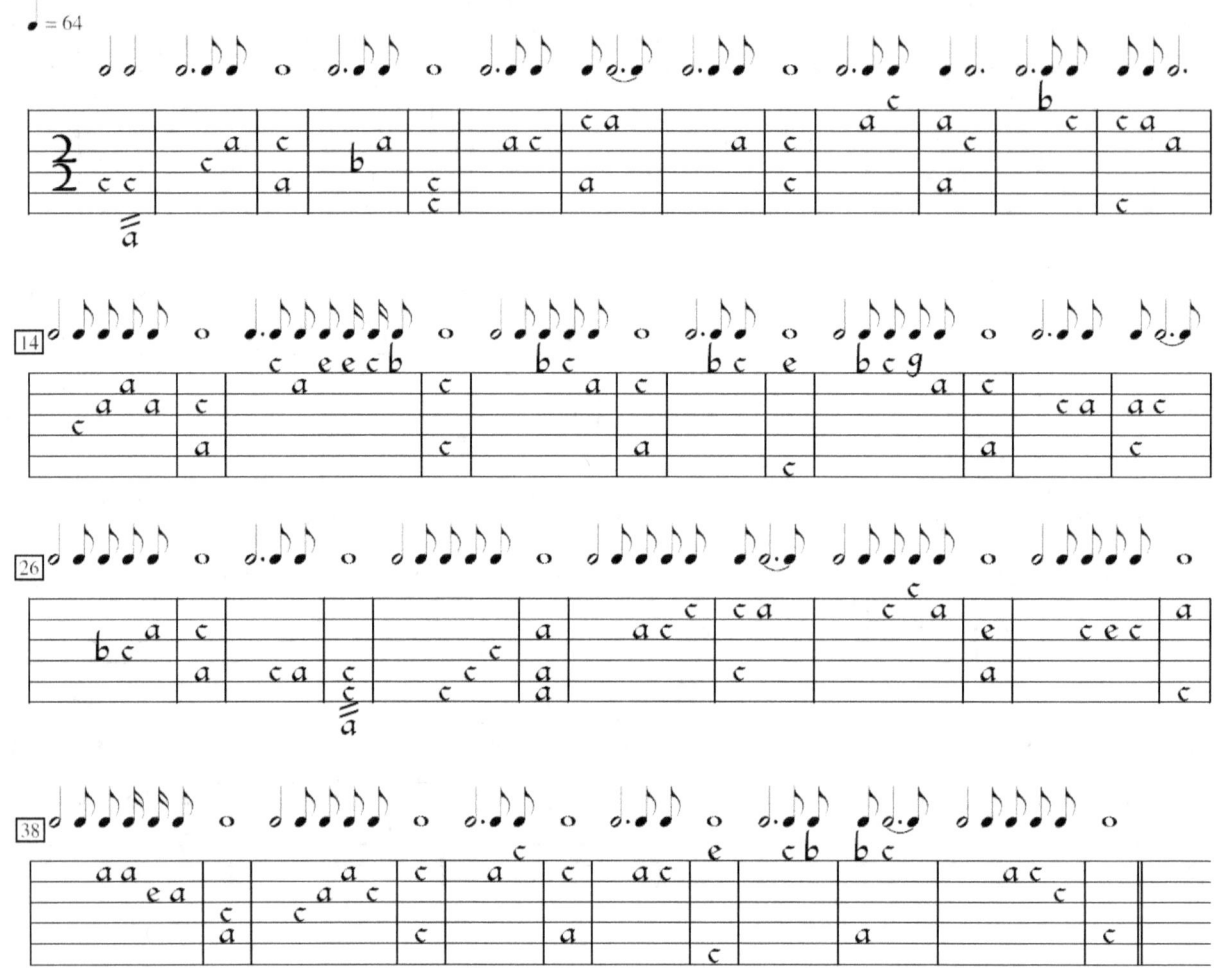

©2012, 2013, 2015, and 2020 Matthew Leigh Embleton

Matthew Leigh Embleton (b1978) — Compositions for Renaissance Lute

Op 12 Late Night Sky in g-minor

Piano molto e penseroso

©2012, 2013, 2015, and 2020 Matthew Leigh Embleton

Matthew Leigh Embleton (b1978) — Compositions for Renaissance Lute

Op 13 Introduction in g-minor

Piano molto e cantabile

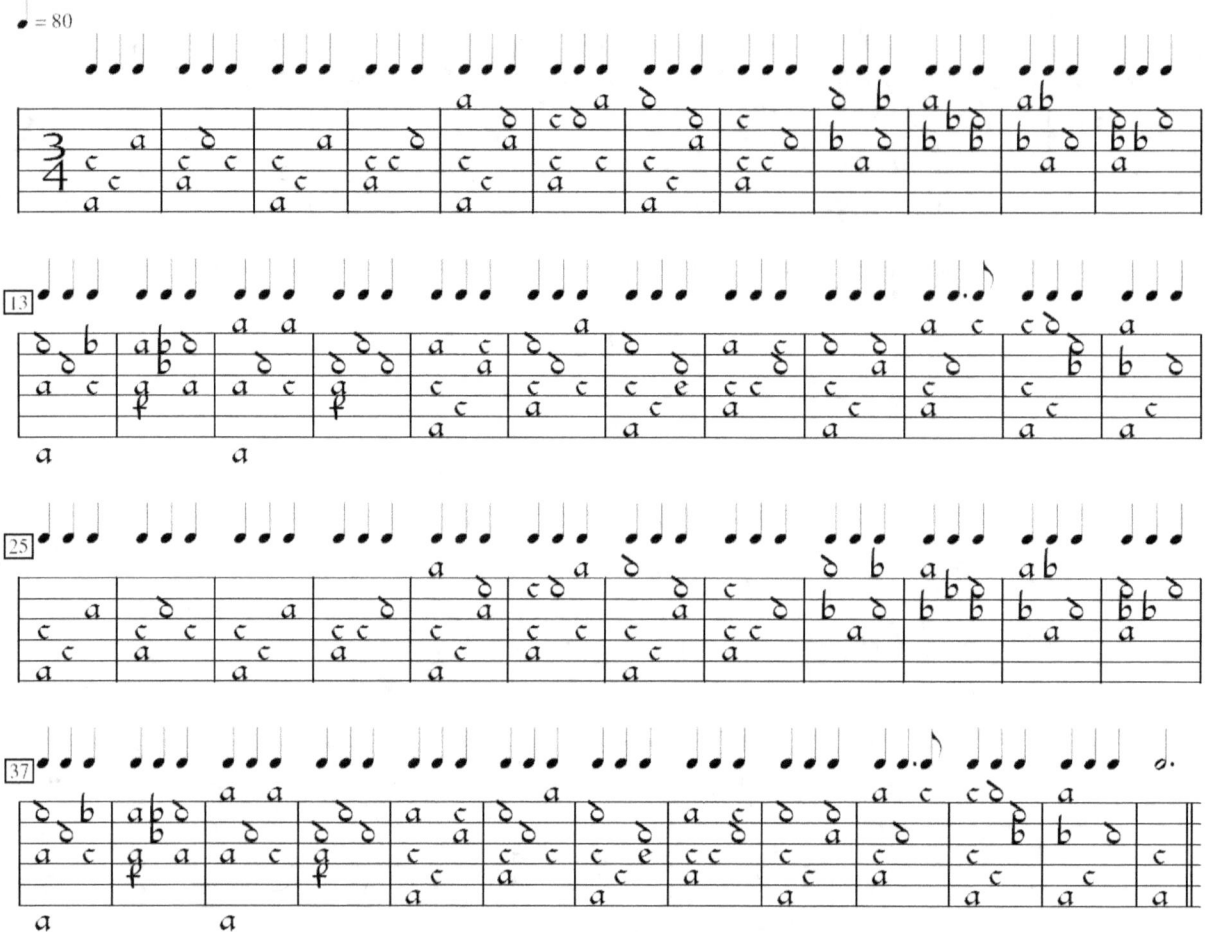

©2012, 2013, 2015, and 2020 Matthew Leigh Embleton

www.ingramcontent.com/pod-product-compliance
Lightning Source LLC
Chambersburg PA
CBHW051428070526
44584CB00023B/3634